This book belongs to:

....

For Elma and Lydia

Written by David Freedman
Illustrated by Mike Kelly

www.stuntcrow.com

From breaking night the morning
brings a wild wind which coughs
five crows from an old oak tree.

The branches reach out
to pull them back.

They scatter,
they drift.
Fluttering like handkerchiefs
caught in the wind.

But one breaks free

and cuts the breeze
which flicks him away.

But he lets it.
He uses it,
he rides with it.

He flies against it.

He is Stunt Crow.

And the heron can only watch

as Stunt Crow scatters shadows
on the lake.

The fox stops.
Stunt Crow drops towards her,

makes her duck
then circles up.

Up he flies
into the whistling skies.

He slices air
with feather knives.
Blue black his wings
push back.

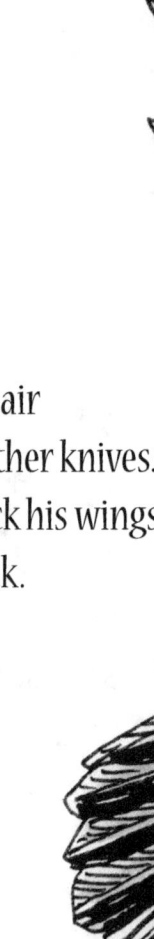

He fights the gust and wins.

And up and up
and up and up

he pushes through
the wild wind,

Into colder softer air

beneath the clouds
which start to rain.

He closes his eyes,

he sleeps as he flies,

Until he rounds the mountain top
where sits the eagle on his rocky throne.

Stunt Crow dares to fly too close.

The eagle screams,
his massive wings outstretched,
and leaps.

His talon rips a feather from the crow
and sends him tumbling in a spin,

but Stunt Crow tucks,
he sweeps,
he ducks.

He turns and climbs.
The eagle circles round behind.
Stunt Crow fears the eagle's eyes
that follow everywhere he flies.

Bigger than him
and faster than him.

Louder than him

...but master of him?

This crow is scared but still he knows
that this fine eagle only goes
where the air is thick,
the bluer sky.

So Stunt Crow turns
to fly up high
where skies are thin
and dark and cold

and the eagle's eye
that flashes gold
follows the crow,

his shrill cry rings,
his muscled back
beats down his wings.

The crow pulls up just glancing back
to feel the eagle's last attack.

A feather falls.
Stunt Crow calls

The eagle stalls.
Upside down he starts to turn.

The air is thin
his muscles burn.

But Stunt Crow keeps on going,
up and up and up and then

As evening breaks
a mile above the Earth,
Stunt Crow curls
into a ball

and the eagle watches as Stunt Crow falls.

He spirals
　　　　　and rolls
　　　and spins
　　　　　　and tumbles.

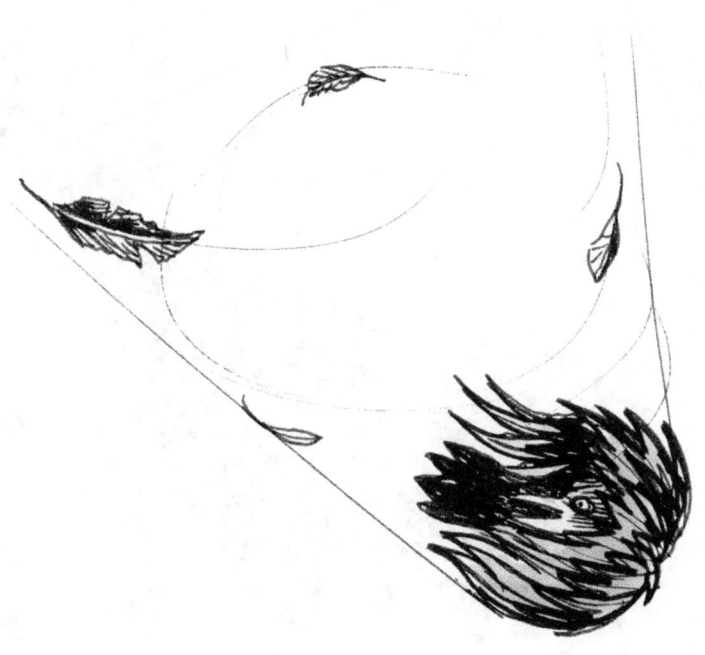

Pigeons scatter

as Stunt Crow smashes clouds.

But Stunt Crow sees the tree
and chops the air in two
with his wing.

He calls out,

RAAAAAAAAK!

With one last spin,

And bends the branch,
his claws dig in.

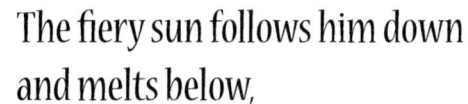

The fiery sun follows him down
and melts below,

And he is back,
and he is bold.

He is Stunt Crow.